THE POETIC EXPRESSIONS OF C.L.P.: CRAZY LOVELY POET

Contact Information:

Email: Mindelevationforall@gmail.com

The Poetic Expressions Of C.L.P.: Crazy Lovely Poet

© 2020

Chanekka Pullens. All Rights Reserved.

Cover art created by Chanekka Pullens

No part of this book may be reproduced or transmitted in any form or by any means, written, electronic, recording, photocopying, or otherwise, without prior written permission of the author, Chanekka LuQuawn Pullens.

Books my be purchased in quantity and/or special sales by contacting the author by email at: mindelevationforall@gmail.com ,with 'Book Purchase' in the subject line

ISBN: 978-1-7355910-1-8

1. Poetry 2. Inspiration 3. Motivation

First Edition

Printed in the USA

To be innocent is not to be naive. To be innocent is not to be fooled. To be innocent is to be kind. To love. To be positive in your life and spread that positive energy to others. To be innocent is to be like our children without the weight of the world.

-Chanekka Pullens

A Letter To My Brothers

This letter is to my brothers,

who art on thy earth and in Heaven.

We've all sinned in this world. I pray to God we're forgiven.

Blood couldn't make us closer. Neither could the death of our oldest brother.

His death broke us all, no one shattered more than our mother.

Then, I couldn't understand what it meant to lose a son personally.

But,

I recently became a mother and the thought of my son leaving me makes my conduct disorderly.

No liquor in my system.

Because I'm not trying to be a lick and get caught in theirs.

So, I'm going to steer with precision,

focus on my vision,

and always remember that Kenny found God,

so, he'll never be missing.

Let's choose to enjoy the beauty in the rainbow, even as we stand in the rain.

Let's choose to look forward to the healing that's inevitable after the pain.

So, to my brothers,

stay strong because I know sometimes the abyss seems like it'll never end.

Although we sent an angel to Heaven, remember that you are Heaven sent.

Five brothers share a brother, two brothers share a father.

They both have a grave missed deeply by their sister and daughter.

Voids that can't be repaid, the world cashed checks our souls can't afford.

But, I'm aboard HER ship, and the only exchange there is through the Bank of the Lord.

I accepted HER payment and I recognize that HER policy is no returns.

And one day SHE will collect on us too, so no concerns.

Just live with Mind Elevation, have faith and hold your own dreams in your hand.

This letter is to my brothers,

who art on thy earth of the Lord.

You're forgiven so get the living.

He's watching!

A Motherless Son

Woke up on a new day to old things.

Trapped on America's hamster wheel.

Is it sad? That I've been saddened, by the fact that we're not healed.

The truth has been suppressed, to the oppressed, let me unseal.

This envelope contains the note, that holds the hope, please hear.

For one second can you listen and understand what's at stake?

Every day that we wait is a day too late.

We take our lives for granted, until death adds to the weight.

That's already placed upon the plate, of the Beautiful Black Race.

Last night a Prince lost his Queen, don't even think he's 8.

Never met her but she was killed by her brotherly hate.

No blood tied them together through life, but through her death, he's permanently stained.

He tried to prove that he didn't play, now he's trapped in the game.

Now, he's in a system that's going to play with him, and he wish he just walked away.

But he can't go back, now he must obey, what big homie say.

But the worst pain he could face, could never replace.

A son who seen his mom last night, but no more days.

Advantage

We take advantage of their love, when their love is here.

We don't believe in magic, until that love disappears.

We don't understand terror, until we've lived our biggest fears.

We don't recognize the power of the smile, until a night of tears.

We don't watch our dreams, television on repeat.

We don't have much, but the lack of 'likes', is what we consider defeat.

We don't get flavor, just the bones, while the whites get the meat.

We don't get to dance, yet we're the ones, who drop the beat.

We don't see, what we can't see, but we're not looking for what can be seen.

We don't understand that all it takes is understanding, for the mind to be keen.

We don't speak the truth to our reflection, Black King and Black Queen.

We don't hear our bloody cries, so we're crying covered in blood, ourselves we demean.

We don't value our lives; we're praised in the grave.

We don't prepare for generational wealth, we spend, we don't save.

We don't create our paths; we travel through the tunnels that's been paved.

We didn't yesterday, but today's a new day.

And we will.

We shall.

Rebirth, new child.

New way, new day.

New judge, new case.

New rule, new school.

New air, a new cool.

New pledge, new ledge.

New words will be said.

New hope will take lead.

New roots from new seeds.

New truths from new dreams.

New river, new stream.

New wealth, new health.

New Us, till there's none left.

Full speed, no seat belt.

All heat, touch will melt.

When we rise, all will fall.
Burn the courts by the balls.
Burn the buildings, burn the Halls.
Break their legs, watch them crawl.

Break their hands, break their necks.
Break their skulls, break their wrists.
Break their knees, take their greed.
Choke them out, they can't breathe.

Take their wealth, take their health.
Take their land, take their help.
Take their lies, take their time.
Take their home, take their lives.

Make them pay, make them wake.
Make them live their mistakes.
Make them see, how we live,
through the eyes of their hate.

And we will overcome, for we shall.
If not for ourselves, then for our child.

Instill in them, "Black Is Royalty". Say loud and proud.

Encourage them to read.
Inspire them to be.
More than us, their future Ancestor's, wildest dreams.

Motivate them to be take advantage,
of the disadvantage, of the disadvantaged.

Embrace the scars after the bandage.
Stand tall even if they can't stand it.
Elevate above and see clearly, refocus before landing.
Peace stealer, peace bandit,
I rebuke you, in English and in Spanish.

And that concludes, Advantage.

Ancestor Apology

I feel like I should,

say it loud, say it strong.

I apologize my Ancestors; I know your descendants living wrong.

Your blood was shed, babies taken.

I thank you for your patience,

and sorry you're still waiting.

My Ancestor's souls are pacing,

back and forth.

They don't understand how we went from being worthy to not knowing our worth.

Deserving of powerful things, but we've never gotten what we deserve.

The price has been paid, it's time to collect, the acres that we've earned.

Now, I want to,

get this out before my casket close.

I need to speak this fire, before the heat gets cold.

I'm glad I listened when the words were spoken.

I could be anything, my destiny could be chosen.

I think I can I be anything that I can see,

and when my third eye opened, I saw the God in me.

My vessel was empty until SHE blew into me HER likeness, you see.

Address me as: God, Black Goddess, Chanekka, or Queen.

Black people please,

achieve our Ancestor's dream.

Look deep in your eye, and discover what life means.

Ase'.

Baby Sister

I was born,

a baby sister.

I was born,

to a big brother.

One son was born before one daughter.

Same mother, different fathers.

Same journey, different path.

Same storm, different aftermath.

Same projects, different trap.

Same beat, different rap.

I was born a baby sister,

to my only big brother.

In life I cherished him so, because I could never have another.

They still call me a snitch, I told as soon as the door opened.

I told because the world, took my father, and my brother couldn't be chosen.

I told because momma was safety, and I wanted him safe.

And momma was safety because when we weren't, she got us out of that place.

She loved her children, so she fought, when they took us away.

Who told that coward to make the day a baby sister was born,

the last day she'd hear her big brother say,

"I love you."

And

"Happy birthday!"

So much cake, on my f*cking plate.

I'm too full,

tummy ache.

Light head, I feel faint.

My pride, been ate.

Justice still late.

System still raped.

He never seen a cell gate.

To never see him, I pray.

Still have the urge to spray, but

I have more to lose than I can say.

So, on this day,

I'll send a prayer up to my big brother.

You're deeply missed by your baby sister.

Bandit

Bearing my heart on my sleeve.
To the one chosen to be my King.
And I'm his Queen,
by any means.

But sometimes in between,
the light doesn't seem to last.
Darkness overshadows our peace,
digging up pain from our past.
Communication is key.
But I'm the only one that gets locked out.
I understand you've lost deeply, but in my lost you have doubt.

God touched your mother,
and my brother answered HIS call.
Instead of that being a reason we stand,
at times that's why we fall.

The father of my seed.
So, in him you're implanted.

When he blooms, I pray he's like his father,

in all ways, except a bandit.

Stole my love.

Stole my mind.

Stole my soul.

Stole my sight.

Love is blind.

Love is music.

Ray Charles playing the Blues.

Will we always overcome the divide

that splits us in two?

Beloved

Dearly departed,
I'm coming fullhearted.

I pray that Heaven Gates opened
with a 'Welcome Home' party.

With, blue balloons,
blue candles,
and blue kisses.

I pray the Lord granted you 23 wishes.
I pray all your sins was washed and forgiven.
Six years today that your body stopped living.
But I know for sure that death isn't the mission.
Your body left, but your spirit transitioned.

You were my protector, no hiding, no witness.
I hear your voice and I listen.
Mind on full, with no dishes.
Get these knives out of my kitchen.

Before, I pick one up, and unleash the demon.
Inside me named revenge. No fetus, no semen.
Excuse my tongue but you get it.
Sometimes my mind gets relentless.
Because he,

murdered my mother's first born in cold blood.
His hands were up. You're a cop's son.

You were arrested then released. No trials, free bond.
Love was killed by hate, yet again hate won.

You only seen a Black King.
But, what about the King's sons?

You probably hoped he'd never multiply,
like your ancestors.

Spread disease and watch them die.
Wait let me catch you.

To say, we won't be defeated.
The kitchen's always been heated.

Although, I never seen fire, until that day you did it.

Let me catch my breath for a minute.

Before I Black Out.

Rest Powerfully to my Black brother.

"Black Power!"

We got the numbers to take over and reach the penthouse.

Call it "Black Towers."

Trump who?

No more tears, soaked tissue.

400 years of collecting debt, America's bills due.

Until then,

to my dearly departed.

I'll see you when I transition, at my

'Welcome Home' party.

We'll share hugs, share laughs, share kisses.

Skip down memory lane, elevate, while reminiscing.

I love you, big brother. I love you Kenny.

Ke'Lonzo Pullens Sr., is forever with me.

Until the day I transition.

Bizarre

Everyone is claiming to be tired.

Funny because everybody is sleeping.

And nobody wants to awaken first.

So, they keep on dreaming.

Lost on the perpetual spinning cotton wheel.

Mental slavery is how they choose to live.

I wouldn't be surprised if we killed more of us in 400 days, than they did in 400 years!

Ironic how they stereotyped us out of fear. And now we fear ourselves most.

But it's the biggest deception in mankind. Yes, our "truth" is a hoax.

Like, I must have straight hair to be beautiful. But there's power in my fro!

Like, he literally must show his a*s, sag, and kill his bro.

More fathers buried and chained, than there are in their kids' lives.

And momma too focused on another brother, whose hands are stained, enslaved by his mind.

Unaware that she has the power to break her family from the perpetual spinning cotton wheel.

Unaware that through GOD, her soul can heal.

And when she heals, her son will.

He'll be raised to walk straight, no need for wheels.

Won't sale his soul for money, close that box, and tell the banker "NO DEAL!"

Then, watch how prosperity wash over his family.

For generations, and that's where we all should want to be.

Promise I'm not ranting I'm just truly exhausted of seeing R.I.P.

But the curse is in the fact, that I can't sleep, so I speak.

And I write, trying to tell you, that royalty is our blood!

Seek the truth, and you'll understand, that our "truth" is a dud.

And I'm unsatisfied by their lies, and I say no more cries!

And I say to my brother, "GUNS DOWN! NO MORE DIES!"

And I say to my sister, "YOU ARE WORTHY, OKAY! THEY LIED!"

Please my people let's choose to awaken, choose Mind Elevation.

We must choose one another, but another choice is what we're making.

Have you seen the world out your window? Do you NOT SEE WHAT'S AT STAKE?!

Please, think about HOW you want to contribute to your future generations.

BEFORE the next move you make.

Black Trauma

The Black Trauma starts with the
Black momma.

Told that we're sheep.
If anything, we're the llama.

And that's word to my momma.
And her mother too.

Gracie wasn't perfect. Nobody fits in those shoes.

Nobody neglects abuse.
We've all been through.

Trials, but the verdict of life is yours.
You're the jury, so choose.

I know Black comes with the Blues.
Suppressed but the oppressor's tools.

Like saying slavery was my start,

redlining and fake news.

Integrated schools,
dumbing down our youth.

Class cancelled every other week for everything
less than the flu.

The truth hurts,
but please hear our truth.

Your heartbeat be the proof.
That you're undefeated,
break into your mind,
and secure the loot.

Secure the treasure,
that your mind holds.

Envision your dreams,
then get up and go!

Only you can manifest,

your divine purpose.

Protect your soul from the world,
it can only touch the surface.

To my Black mothers,
you are more than worth it.

You are the creators,
of this world,
and you're deserving.

Of true love.
Of true peace.
You're no b****,
need no leash.

Your reflection,
you must teach,
your voice, to rise,
and speak.

Defend her, let her defend you.

You see who the warriors were, in the Wakanda movie.

Blend all the hate, drink it like a smoothie.

Turn it into energy, and keep it moving.

And at the day's end, relax your mind,

it's soothing.

Read a book,

maybe watch a movie.

Just remember before you go to bed.

Today is the gift, yesterday's the past.

Tomorrow is the chance,

to rise again.

Hand in hand.

Bloody Contract

Silence is poison.

Once bitten you will submit.

To the voices of snakes, that seem to forget.

That if you open your mind,

elevate, and learn the truth.

Their bite won't phase you.

Yes, knowledge is the venom, and I'm the proof.

See, they lurked in the grass,

on the side that looked greener.

Greener grass,

greener money,

greener you. Your envy got meaner.

So, you wanted an invite.

They say,

"Sure. But be quiet.

Over here you're mine.

So, don't speak, don't read, and you

better not dare use your mind.

But you can have all the money and fame that you like.

Just put your thumb right here, with your blood on this line.

Finally, you must portray to the world nothing but ignorance.

Go on TV and degrade your people in front of your children.

You must make sure the generational curse we placed on your people, never be broken.

And don't worry if you get in trouble, Trump is in our back pocket.

No, he wasn't elected but chosen.

You just make sure that you pull your people down.

While we push down from the top.

But if you consider all the money. This isn't really asking a lot."

End quote.

So, you signed your name.

Sold your soul to the game.

Only in the end to find out,

that the grass wasn't even green.

You see, money was thrown around, covering the

cemetery underneath.

You lived your life to the illusion,

that you couldn't be great for who you are.

You feed the perceptions of the world.

But let your mind starve.

So, before you shoot the messenger.

Open your mind, elevate, and learn the truth.

Knowledge is the venom, and my proof is

in my books.

Bloody Roots

Have I not sacrificed?

Are the things I've done not enough?

Sometimes I feel my mental slipping, yet my mind is numb when it's touched.

You'd think when I lost my brother, we'd be even.

Yet, at times I feel like you won't meet me half-way. Not even 50/50.

Don't get me wrong I know that you've never left my side.

Yes, you're always with me.

Ironic because I feel alone like a single wall, and the world is against me.

Now, if 'you' just hush your ignorance. For a single minute.

Your 3rd eye will be much clear, forehead sight no longer tinted.

And no, I haven't lost my thought,

just stating facts while you're still with me.

Because soon you'll leave like we all must, ashes to dust.

So, I keep the flowers in me.

Repeat,

So, I keep the flowers in me,

before they're placed above.

Before I transition from this temporary, and all that's left is who I was.

And I pray that on that day, I would have had walked far enough.

To move the scale for my great great great great grandkids, to survive off of love.

To survive off the truth.

To reject all abuse.

To stand proud when they think of their Ancestor, who provided the proof.

Who took back the loot.

Who learned how to shoot.

Who planted the seeds of sacrifice,

blood in our roots.

Class In Session

Still waiting on freedom to ring.

I guess class is still in session.

I mise of well take a seat and receive a lesson.

It couldn't hurt for me to hear the message.

Maybe teach can tell me why I'm stressing,

By the fact, the skin in which I was born is considered a weapon.

And he better not continue those lies,

truth still resting.

You'd think that we'd be ready to be stronger after 400 plus years

of being "inferior" injected.

We deserve to be protected.

Even to ourselves we've neglected.

Less of my people have "freedom",

even more are arrested.

And even more Blacks are buried.

Heavenly kisses to mom's first Black son.

Rest heavenly to my Black brothers killed by the black gun.

Pray to the heavens my Black people, I know being Black's not all fun.

But if it wasn't for the Black womb, no life would have begun.

No song would be sung.

No breath in no lungs.

No KKK, No AK's, No hate and no guns.

No system, no prez.

No life, all dead.

No cult, no red.

No wine, no bread.

*Ringggggggggggggggg

Culture And Vultures

This poem is for the culture, and
the vultures.

For the ones laying the brick,
and launching the boulders.

Feel like the world's on my shoulders.
Feel like I may sink.
Sometimes my sight loses focus, and
all I have is my think.

All I have is mind.
Heart locked down doing time.
That means murder got us paralyzed.
Time to plan and organize.

It's time to strategize.
How we're going to survive.
The strongest is the last one standing every time.

Ten toes down, one dime.

One dime gets him Ten.

3650 days enslaved, away from his kids.

Man's biggest sin,

is choosing who wins.

Is choosing who starts,

and choosing who end.

Just give me my dividends,

for the blood put in.

For the enslavement, and murder of my kin.

Give me my voice, keep the Benz.

Check ya mate,

I win.

My culture is appreciated, except the color of my skin.

By the vultures.

Dear Life

I know that you're temporary, for everything that is born.

I know that you're hard, and sometimes can't be won.

And I say that because suicide is real. I almost quit more than once.

You were beating me down, stole my crown, and I felt like I had no choice.

See Life, you only made me one promise, and that is that our relationship is temporary.

And you promised me that you would be harder for me for some time, because I was born a Blacker berry.

You said, "But that doesn't mean no sweeter juice. For you or nobody like you.

You can wake any day and be full of me but, lose me just because he want to shoot."

And I'm sad to say that you're right. Like always, like my mother.

Now, I'm writing this letter to you, for being temporary for 23 years.

For the you she started, my brother.

The day he lost you, I almost did too. Only did his voice save me.

And that made 29 because each year of you for me, another emerges, guess society would call me crazy.

But you know, the objective of this letter, isn't to curse you about the bad things.

It's to say, I appreciate the temporary opportunity; because without you I couldn't be anything.

And yes, you told me that you were temporary. Trust me I learned with my dad at 4 and Chris in the 8th grade.

But I appreciate you every day because we were kids then. I learned that you'll leave at any age.

This letter could be perpetual, but I would like to conclude before you leave me.

Let me go live you, before I Rest In Peace.

Fake News

Fake news creates real tools,
apply real pressure and pay real dues.
Corrupt real minds, cost real time.
Stuck on a loop, no lines.

Fake news, I realize
was created to internalize.

Their hate, through their eyes.
Like, being Black is no prize.

Like, Black has a bitter taste.
A quarter less of the human race.

Like, Black is born in last place.
Black's evolve at a slower pace.

Fake news, I understand.
Is owned by the white man.
By the white team,
for the white dream.

Make my coffee black, no cream.

No pleas, no screams.

Guns down, no more bleeds.

Books up, please more read!

Hope more with more dreams.

Believe you can and be.

Leave hate alone and see.

You are more than a damn tool!

And what you see on the fake news.

So,

No lies.

No more cries.

Soul shout, "No more dies!"

No more march, now we ride.

By any means, X, out the other side.

Fake news, I conclude.

You're used to dilute.

My history and my truth.

My name and my roots.

Foundation

I'm going to lay the foundation with my hands.

To make sure you have a foundation to stand.

Because the foundation they've laid, is no foundation for a Black man.

Because the foundation they've built for you,

allows Black hands to be up and they shoot.

The foundation they laid, makes you believe you were founded as slaves and it's not true.

They replaced our crowns with mind chains,

even erased our Great names.

If we continue to stand on the foundation they've laid, at the bottom we'll remain.

It's the responsibility of the parents, to lay a proper foundation for our seeds.

It's the responsibility of the parents, to raise Kings and Queens.

It's the responsibility of the parents, to guide your children to Greatness.

It's the responsibility of the parents to walk forward and stop waiting.

I'm going to lay the foundation for you my son. To make sure that you make it.

Because for you to only live on their foundation, hell no, they're mistaken.

I'm going to keep my three eyes open. Your success is my focus.

Refuse to let the world take my baby and use your grave as a token.

Because they better believe that if momma can't, then daddy is toting.

Us on his shoulders, and on my back, the weapon is loaded.

I'm going to lay the foundation with my hands. To make sure you have a foundation to stand.

Because nothing is more scary yet rewarding. Than loving and raising a Black man.

Full Speed

Her journey hasn't been easy, and neither has mine.

But we've been riding together, surviving side by side.

We became two different women, because of our mothers.

Three separate generations forever tied together because of our struggles.

Her mother chose drugs, making her a mother before she laid.

Down with a boy and became a mother again.

A beautiful young flower couldn't bloom. She was picked from her garden before she was ready.

Instead of getting the sun outside to thrive, she was at home watching, "Ed, Edd n Eddy".

Two children holding on to her ankles, we stayed at her feet, bowing to our Queen.

Even then we saw her true beauty, although her eyes couldn't be seen.

She became a mother of two when she was just 16.

Plus, four in the next few years, eventually five Kings and one Queen.

Now, let's move at a fast pace, to my roots and my base.

To my blood, my kin, my Queen, my best friend.

My heart, my soul, our bond is my goal.

For my son, my seed. I will achieve that by any means!

As she did by herself. With no man and no help.

On her back I stepped.

So, I could climb over even if she got left.

In this life she sacrificed.

I wouldn't lie and say she did it all right.

She fell short and stumbled, but she never stayed down.

She knew she couldn't tell me I had one, if she didn't pick up her crown.

And if she didn't, I did.

Dusted it off for her and put it back on.

Held her hand, helped her up, and said get back on your throne.

You see, I can't pass the kingdom to my son, if it's not passed to me.

A King can't become King, if there's no Queen.

I pray I mean as much to my son as you mean to me.

Our journey hasn't been easy, but in every life count me in

    Full Speed.

Furthermore

I was burned, from ashes to dust.

From which I came.

A Black Phoenix rose, when I was reborn with my name.

Reincarnated, soul tied to my Ancestral spirits.

And this I know, and because of this, someone's livid.

Because of this they place restrictions on my living.

Furthermore, they place those limits on our children.

Furthermore, slavery never died, he still living.

From his balls, he multiplied through his children.

Mother spoke hate, she neglected the healing.

So, hate rises, elevates, no ceilings.

Money over life, life is numbered, live for billing.

No more Black fish in the sea, stop reeling!

Stop killing.

Stop stealing.

Stop raping.

Start hearing.

Start loving.

Stop hating.

Stop judging me first, start waiting.

Don't rush, be patient.

Furthermore, for the racists.

I am worth more,

than you can pay me.

Future Of The Fruitful Female

The future is female.

If you can't tell.

Because it's been a man's world, trapped in a hot hell.

Waiting on freedom to ring, it's time to ring the bell.

Time for smooth sentences to be spoken,

not yell.

It's time to rehabilitate with hope, not cells.

It's time to repel.

The lies that they tell.

It's time to find faith in the fruitful female.

The future shall be founded by the fruitful, let me tell.

The future is depending on my history.

No ships, no mails (males).

It's time for Queens to rise and save ourselves.

It's time to protect our children with the strength of Love's shield.

It's time to pick up the debris and rebuild.
It's time to hold hands and watch us heal.

They said the future can't be seen.
Well, we're right here.

No more migrating from our land, trail of tears.
I'll wipe yours with my heart, and uplift.
My fellow females.

The future's cards are in our hands, no re-deal.
Fortified from their fear, yet we're feared.
Man ignore my brain, only see on my rear.

So, I stay covered, like they shooting.
They gone hear me today, til' I'm ozzing.

Out of my body, I'd rather speak, live in peace.
There's no option to be weak.
If we create life, we can sustain it.

Tired of being exhausted, no more patience.
Females can do more than create babies.

We can be the President.

We can rule the world.

Nothing more fulfilling than being born a girl.

Love to my females, FEM:

First Embodiment of Mankind.

Love to my Queens, rising to the grind.

Love to the mothers. Both married and single.

No holidays needed, this a daily jingle.

No bells, shoot all shells, at all those that tell.

Me I'm only my body and nothing else.

I bet a female will cure cancer.

I bet a female bring forth world peace.

Love to my women, say it with me.

"The future is female."

"The future is female."

Say it loud and proud.

Drive all the men wild.

Tell your man you're more, than the mother of his child.

You can own the business, I'm a witness.

You can bring more to the table, not just wash the dishes.

Signed, a female of the future.

And you can call this here, a sutra.

Does it make you think?

Where would the world be?

If the world was the ruled, by the Queens?

No worries though, here soon it will be.

I see the vision, so the vision, I speak.

Love, a fruitful female.

Ase'.

Harley

Sometimes, I feel like I can't survive.

But I don't think that makes me weak.

I believe that the pressure comes from the height,

when you're reaching your peak.

Momma lost a child,

me and my brothers are one brother short.

I can't voluntarily take my life.

When he had no choice.

Although sometimes I feel like I'm going crazy.

No, I wonder, or maybe.

But crazy like The Joker and Harley Quinn had a baby.

Pig tails with a planted smile, descendant going wild.

Acting a donkey, straight clown, makes my parents proud.

Wait, let me calm down.

Adjust my crown.

Remind my reflection, I'm the Lioness, and let out a growl.

Let out a howl, wolf sh*t, like I'm Jacob.

Conceal my scars, no makeup.

My team will win, and my son's the Most Valuable Player.

So, the vampires, I'll slay them.

Use Edward's hands.

To cut the noose, around my neck.

Use it to hang the man.

Amen.

More Than

I am more than a woman.

I am more than super.

I write more than books, I provide Sutras.

I am more than my age.

Opened my eye, so my Ancestors could speak.

Then I listened, and they said, "You're everything but weak."

Black Queens said, "Believe it or not, but it started with me.

And they gone tell you that you can only be, what they say to be."

Integrated societies were formed, so we could conform, and never confirm our story.

And it being untold is the greatest agony, proclaimed Queen Maya, and to God be the glory.

I am more than a woman.

I am more than a mother.

I didn't only create life; I created a brother.

I created a Prince, who shall one day be a King.

Who shall one day roar, and even the jungle will clear the scene.

Who shall one day stand,

as his mother hold his hand.

As he looks up to his father,

who always told him he can.

And we'll tell him that he will,

blaze trails, all fire, no chill.

So, we grind while he crawls.

So, when he run, he focus on the race, and not the bills.

I am more than a woman.

I am more like a Queen.

I love more than a man; I love a king.

And we have more than worldly love, God intervened.

Never can we broken, protected by any means.

Yes, I am more with him.

But I'm even more with me.

I am a mother then woman.

Sincerely, Black Queen.

My Beautiful Creation

You were created from my life.

So, my life, I give unto you.

Your beautiful grey eyes give me sight when my sight's down to two.

Not ashamed to admit, my fore-eye sometime closes,

my mind loses its focus.

But God implanted me with such a seed, that I must remember,

I wasn't elected but chosen.

To be your mother on this earth, guide your soul thus your spirit.

I promise to prove to you that it's more to life than just living.

You will understand that your peace of mind and your soul

are the keys to a smoother transition.

By that I mean who you are while you're going through it, is who you are at the end your mission.

I promise, you'll never be missing,

as the Lord is my witness.

Laying your foundation with my hands, building a business.

So, you'll never have to depend on the business, where they can make the call.

To fire and hire when they want, don't care if you fall.

So, for my son I'll ball.

Back and forth down the court.

For my son, I'll chew my problems and swallow my hurt.

My sun you're so much more valuable, than this world is worth.

But the world your mother will give you. Because from her you were birthed.

And I get my life unto you.

God blessed me, achoo.

With you, my beautiful son.

Mommy loves you.

One: Thirteen

Does he deserve it or not?

Sometimes I don't know.

He drives me half crazy. Is it crazy he makes me whole?

He's full of flaws, but I'm filled with imperfections.

I believe with him I shall prosper, love being his weapon.

He tries to give his heart, although his biggest piece is missing.

And I don't know what to say, knowing I can't give him what he's wishing.

Four months feels like an eternity in the depts of his mind.

Hate to admit I sometimes don't see his tears as mine fills my eyes.

I remember when I first saw him, hazel eyes took my soul.

Not saying it was love at first sight, but that was six years ago.

I wouldn't fix my mouth to say it's been easy.

This ride has been high and low at a fast pace, roller coaster making us dizzy.

Even if we wanted out 100%; we're in 50/50.

For a King was born, as a Queen made her transition.

I'm blessed that she instilled in me some pieces that was missing.

I promise my heart is still ripped as the Lord is my witness.

We both put too much on our plate, not wanting to do dishes.

So, we're both weighed down on the inside, with only two plates in the kitchen.

When there should be three, A King, and Prince, and a Queen.

It's literally impossible to be together when there's space in between.

So, does he deserve it or not? Yes, maybe, or no?

I'll run and kick any object in the way, their happiness is my goal!

So, no, neither of them deserves it, and neither do I.

We must defeat our opponents, to have victory and the prize.

Only, if he understood that if he could only wipe mine from my eyes,

then I could see his tears,

and together we'll rise.

And heal.

Pissed

I can't be pissed.

So, I sit.

Sometimes the source of my strength comes when I reminisce.

About the ones I miss.

Remembering that final kiss.

On that last day I'll ever see them, I pray they never forget.

That they're truly missed.

Oh', shit!

I've cried so many tears, there's no more liquid,

only mist.

So, I do this.

With my wrist.

Write my pain, then put my pain down, and raise my fists.

Instead of being pissed.

Queen Maya

I hear them complain about the game.

Temporarily paralyzed by the fact that the world hasn't changed.

Still in shock when the Black man selling cigarettes or carrying skittles get killed.

And the white ones whose killing Blacks and students are still here.

Almost every Black person I know feels the anger this cause.

Yet, we steady fantasize outside of reality. We've left Kansas, we're in Oz.

We'd rather write a post and share the message that we need help.

Instead of going outside, being vocalized, and save ourselves.

The fact that we kill us, and they do, has numbered our souls.

Queen Maya said it best, still we should rise, so I rose.

Like D, defense, to defend our lives because like me,

you too are worthy and your life matter.

So, you can either physically take a stand, or continue to sit in silence.

Now, together let's gather, and

rise with the Queen.

Rise

Had a Black son by my Black man.

My Black Prince and my Black King.

Pray one day I don't have to "act Black" and make more than freedom ring.

Because we're living in a world, where he was judged before he entered.

Only thing the world see is another "gangster n*gger."

Even though I never had to say free his dad, and he never had to say free me.

And before he was created, we put in time and love and got our degree.

But the only thing the world would see, is his outer appearance.

The white world doesn't understand our language, yet we're the ones that's incoherent.

See all we speak for is peace, justice, and a chance.

Don't understand how in 400 years we're still begging,

on our knees, holding out our hands.

And all they give us are scraps, jail time, and a mass grave.

Unfortunately, this won't stop until we break their mental chains

and rise.

Sacrifice

I heard somebody ask her, "Do you think your brother was the sacrifice that got you this far?"

The question blew me back, and I started thinking, that I believe that you are.

Domino effect, the chain of events, that got me standing here feeling sick.

Bottles became my best friends searching for a genie, to grant me just one wish.

I hope you know that I apologize, and I want to cry more, but my eyes dry.

I shouldn't feel so guilty by the fact that I dreamed, something told me not to go to sleep.

Had dreams to be more, make momma proud, and you too.

But if I never dozed off, I would have taken the bullet when he chose to shoot.

I promise I wouldn't have thought twice. You had two seeds to bloom, and I had none.

I understand the pain of being fatherless as a daughter. Will it be harder as a fatherless son?

Crazy because in life I've met death. Remember, we saw his brains on the concrete?

Even then I knew death was the end of life, but I never thought death you would meet.

So, was I naïve or in denial, that you could never leave me here?

The thought was so far out of my mind, it was not on my list of fears.

And that's exactly why my soul rocked, disintegrated my insides.

Stomach came up, knees broke down, my first thought was suicide.

But YOU told me, "NO!" right then. But damn, best friend.

You were my other side my entire life. But now I'm just left, and it's not right.

I knew and I know I must stay strong.

Couldn't let that B*tch take two of her children with one bullet.

So, I wrote my pain inside these books, and I quit making excuses.

I made the choice to elevate because this world would be the reason I deflate.

And I made the choice to control my mind, because it's such a terrible thing to waste.

Everything happens by Gods hands. And HE just so happened to need you.

HE knew that I would break to my lowest low because I did too.

But SHE can't make you like new, if nothing is broken, so SHE snapped me.

And SHE built me back up and I hope you're happy that I'm happy.

I've accepted HIS call because one day I will be the one to answer.

And when I meet HER, we'll have a full house, no Tanners.

Ke'lonzo Deontez Pullens Sr., your only sister really miss you.

Your sacrifice won't be in vain, like how we shouldn't use HER name.

Amen.

Seis

Heart numb, heart break.

Heart pierced by the stake.

By the pain,

by the tears.

Can't believe it's been six years.

Since you left, gained your wings.

Heart dripping down my sleeve.

Arm soaked, stained red.

Mind trapped by what you said.

Mental repeat, hearing you speak.

Saying you know who I can be.

Who I would, who I should.

When I didn't know, you understood.

Beneath me, you help raise,

me up on my down days.

When I slip and deflate.

When I forget to elevate.

When my sane comes second, and the in comes first.

On those days, I look up, and remember this verse.

Shed a tear remembering my brother in the back of the hearse.

Heart numb, but it's still beating, so it could be worse.

And I know your spirit is elevated, on me you're patiently waiting.

Trust, that I will be successful in your name, and raise our babies.

We got us.

Self-Reflecting

As I stare at my reflection, I search deep inside.

For only I hear the silent cries I cry.

Only I understand the battles and the wars that has been fought.

And only I know the lessons, that these scars has taught.

Memory lane I'm speeding down, and

sometimes I don't want to be around.

Nobody,

because I might swerve, and I'm the only one who should drown.

Well, I am.

Tidal waves of regret. No matter how hard I fight,

try to catch my breath.

I can't.

I'm light head.

Still can't believe that they dead.

The last words that they said.

Keeps me up, no sleep, no bed.

Shoot,

no room, no house.

Pain numbed, no ouch!

But every day I hop up and carry myself, no pouch.

And that reference was to a Kangaroo, in case you didn't know what I was talking bout'.

Anyways,

My reflection got me reflecting. Mirror rigged like the election.

Because what I've been through, you can't see.

And I thank my Lord for that blessing.

Shakespeare

To be or not to be.
Blinded or to see.

Moving or stay still.
Awoke or asleep.

To be who you're meant to be.
Or to be who they said.

To be the baker baking.
Or the beggar of the bread.

The owner of the land.
Or out in the field.

It's impossible for flowers to bloom,
in soil that's not healed.

The soul can't be killed.
Even as the body burn.
Even as you raped our Kings in front of their Queens.

You hoped we'd fucking learn.

To accept,
   white hate,
    white lies.

Blacks fucked by white guys.
While Blacks cried,
Blacks died.

White hell,
no white prize.

In this white race.
White house, white courts.
This is a white place.
Ever since it was stolen on that first day.

Intended to harm, as
"I'll help." Is what they say.

Not surprised blood it costs, when blood's
the bricks that they laid.

Making messes they don't clean.
Guess I'm the Black maid,

in the black chain.
Locked up in the black cage.

This is Black rage.
Black work, Black don't get paid.
I guess Blacks are slaves.

Not.
To be or not to be.
The decision is yours.
Either you're outside with King Nat planning.
Or in Massa' house doing chores.

Either you're a piece of the puzzle,
that shall complete us,
or you're misleading.

Keep your mind's eye open.
Stay woke while you're dreaming.

My Ancestor's sacrifice,

from my Ancestor's bleeding.

Will not be in vain, every day I'm achieving.

Every day that I rise,

elevate above their hate.

Elevate above the limits

and the boundaries they place.

Every day when I look at my reflection,

I see my Greats looking back.

So, I look forward,

and that's the Black fact.

Ase'.

Social Definitions

Everybody wants to live longer, but nobody wants to age.

Apply makeup and anti-age, desire to remain at 21 years and one day.

Everybody wants the apple bottom, without doing a squat.

Apply injections to their imperfections, unaware of when too much is a lot.

We blame social conditions and social pressure.

But society isn't the best, and you must want to personally do better.

My imperfection is that I'm a little crazy. Tell me, what's yours?

Sometimes, like Miquel, you have to say, "Self, I adore."

But can I tell you the intentions,

of social definitions.

Basically, they were placed to perpetuate,

systematic racism and straight out hate.

We consciously accept, everything they say,

as the truth.

We accept their lies, even as we see evidence and the proof.

Everybody's the same, society's box is the ceiling.

Individuality's missing.

Change is there, but nobody's willing.

To initiate change, become a diamond from the pressure,

of societal standards.

Society's diseases spread, curable like cancer.

But humanity is Prancer,

Rudolph is the big PHARM.

Greed leads, more bleeds.

Hospitalized for a cold, leave with one arm.

Side effects cause more harm,

than the illness itself.

Society's definition of living, is working then death.

The cost of our health,

are billions of dollars.

Billions of sons. Billions of daughters.

Billions are murdered. Billions are slaughtered.

In a society built on blood, shed by your founding fathers.

The Thought Of Him

I often find myself crying.

The loneliness my soul feel.

I listen to HER words and pray to be healed.

Trying to fight the current, but I'm steady drowning.

I try to tell myself I will overcome,

but if I don't, did I allow it?

If the thought of my son can't defeat the tears.

Will he have to witness momma weep through the years?

Because I remember my mother's tears and at times

that contributes to mine.

So, will I make my son better?

Or without me will he be fine?

I can only pray that he grows to be stronger than me.

I can only pray that I didn't pass my curse down to my seed.

The curse of:

self-doubt, self-hate, and self-destruction.

I pray that if I'm defeated, he doesn't think that he's worthless.

Because the moments of peace, of happiness, the days I feel healed.

The only brightness through my clouds is the thought of him.

    My sun.

This Is America

This is America,
the home of the free.

The place where you're rewarded,
when Blacks don't breathe.

The star-spangled banner,
was written, as he loved upon his slaves.

America's the home of the free,
for the ones who hasn't paid.

For the ones who hasn't laid,
but the ones who rape.

Fuck humanity without a condom,
and look what they made.

Trials, Tribulations, and Trump.
Keeping us in the back, in the trunk.

We can't breathe, we can't say see.
Just praying for luck.

Praying to the white man, to deliver us from
the white hell.

From the black grave, from the black cell.
Freedom still hasn't rung,
at least not the Black bell.

No convictions, modern day lunching.
Killer cop awarded paid leave and a pension.

America's decisions,
got me livid.

The revolution's been televised, we're just not hearing.
Headphones while we drive, not focused, just steering.
Don't matter where we end up, no damns given to Black children.

Only value is after life, Black heart sold on the Black market.

Black lungs for the white people, bidding at the Black auction.

Black kids keep come up missing, piling up, like dirty dishes.

Skinned and torn apart, Black skin end up in ditches.

I know this is hard to imagine,

but life's no fairytale, no Alladin.

But my dreams are in the stars,

I elevate and go grab it.

Told that "Black is tragic",

but Black Is Black magic.

Black is royalty, televised as ratchet.

Role models get disrespected,

unaware of the weapon.

Encouraging our kids,

to be born, live, and die,

fully naked.

Our truth should be protected.

Please, stop your children from learning corrupt lessons.

This Morning

I take a deep breath to start my day.

Inhale and exhale, then I tell the Lord, "Thank you.

I'm blessed to see another day."

Then, I send my prayers up to my angels.

See last night I cried, and I don't apologize.

I'd rather let the pain out.

I'd rather shed the pain in the dark, for joy comes in the morning with no doubts.

And when the pain washes away, I praise my Lord name!

For touching my broken heart day by day.

And making a way!

I make a choice to elevate my mind.

Before SHE elevates my soul.

So, if you see me take a deep breath through the day; it's because I rose,

    this morning.

Through Time

100 years shall pass after me, just as 100 years before.

So, this letter is to me, from my roots and my core.

If I happen to read this, on the year I'm resurrected.

I'm telling myself to live by it, and by it I shall be protected.

One, never lose your peace of mind, never leave your elevation to chance.

Two, never stop moving, if you can't walk; dance.

Three, listen to your tune, the melody of your soul.

Four, never forget that what was once young, must become old.

Either in life or in death, birthdays are celebrated.

That's why sometimes I move too fast, and I have my patience waiting.

Because when my hair turns grey, either <u>on</u> land or <u>in</u> a grave.

The only day and time that we will ever be in, is in that time on the day.

You see, either time has passed, thus the past,

or time is to come, thus the future.

The only present is right now, and my present right now, is in his booster.

Honestly, my gift forever.

To my future self, you have a son.

In this life you had battles, every single one you won.

In this life you were an author, you wrote books to elevate.

You dedicated your life to prove that the mind is a terrible thing to waste.

To my future self, I do understand that 100 years has passed.

But my roots and my core shall last.

Through Time.

To My Love

I've written my love out to you before.

But I feel that this one needs to be special.

And I'm going to bare my heart,

cracking down, yolk spilled. But no walking on eggs shells.

Seashells by the seashore.

I love you more, than I damn near love myself.

Because you still buy me after you try me.

If love's free, why are we paying to get the wealth?

And sometimes you're bad for my mental health.

But we're right, and it'll be wrong if we went left.

No U turns, or reverse, in this life, so, hop in and buckle your seat belt.

We'll stay in our own lane, at our own pace, we're the only three in our race.

Always put ya'll first, like before a meal, you better bow your head and say grace.

I love your handsome face, your hazel got me captive, no escape.

But what I need from you is understanding, right here and today.

See, I need you to comprehend,

that your love gets me higher than a tower, no twins.

And for you, I'll shed the blood of my Father's kids, no kin.

When I first saw you, I turned completely, six years later, I spin.

Desire your love, lust for your soul, yes, you are my sin.

Ironically, you're my blessing.

And you're mine for this life, no asking.

Humbled to have bloomed your beautiful flower, from the seed that you planted.

Grateful that your mother witnessed you become a father, before our Father handed.

Her set of wings, she flew up, I know in Heaven she landed.

Even through your worst nightmare, you're still my biggest dream.

I promise to love you through my life, cause in death she gave you to me.

I gave her my word, that I would take care of her son and our son.

We're three individuals, but we come together as one.

You're far from perfect, and sometimes I may be further.

But together, we created perfection, thank you for making me a mother.

You're the perfect father, I know your mother is proud.

Whenever you miss her, just smile up, cause she's smiling down.

Truth Be Told

Truth be told, this shit is old.

Royalty's been off the throne.

For too long.

It's time for us to get back to where we belong.

To come home,

mentally.

We must awaken, to discover, and behold.

Our history, our truth, the price.

You wouldn't be here if someone gave up and quit the fight.

Your blood is as rich as you could believe, you have no right.

To piss on the price of the priceless sacrifice.

There's too much pain,

and not enough healing.

Not many fathers, but too many children.

More funerals, less graduations, is what I'm attending.

I'm daydreaming,

I'm meaning.

I dream during the day.

No night needed.

No dark, no shade.

Where there's a will, there's a way.

It's time to wake.

Because truth be told, our truth's on hold.

The truth we must take.

Our future is what we make.

In the future our truth will be told.

Our truth will be the way.

Black no longer scold.

Waiting

We're being murdered in our face, forehead turning a blind eye.

We're waiting for people to be sorry, who don't know how to apologize.

We're waiting for a system to change, that's only operating from its foundation.

We have patience for the bullshit, but for unity we have no patience.

The world is operated by racists.

Sorry, but I had to say it.

1% owns 99%. Yet, we're the ones that's paying.

We're the ones slaving,

mindless behaving.

Their goals are achieved when they lock us in cages.

When our voices aren't say-less.

They wire our mouth, no braces.

The point is to keep us a full bill, no tips, no changes.

So, no more waiting.

Freedom is mine. Freedom is yours.
It's in your vote, it's in your voice.

You have a say in representation, you have a choice.
I rolls up, no Royce.
Elevate, above the limits on us.
I can't wait, much at stake.
To my people, much love.

Warrior Or Worrier

Are you a warrior or a worrier?

First, let me tell you the difference.

Either you're the running the game,

or getting run with it.

Either you're loyal to a fault, to which I'm a personal witness.

I've caught many friends holding the knife with my blood,

but I never got caught with it.

And I never got caught with it. Because I've never picked it up.

I never betrayed even as I laid, in my own blood.

So, either you're loyal to a fault.

Or your loyalty has no halt.

Which means you're the silly slug creeping every which way

you're led by the salt.

I don't think you know that eating too much salt will kill you.

And yes, I know that we all shall pass away.

But you're a worrier if you're too worried about what the next has to say.

About somebody who is not there at that time and at that place.

If it's that's deep I'm sure you can see them and say it to their face.

This world has become a place,

where you can write checks,

that your ass don't have to pay.

Run up credit, go in debt, then you're bankrupt.

Monopoly's last place.

Monopolies owned by four names.

Four families rule everything.

But anybody can get rich, making money from the slave trade.

Warrior blood in my veins.

Warrior blood shall remain.

Lock the worriers down,

links in their chain game.

Waterfall's Current

I remember the site of the waterfall.

Beautiful streams crashing to a violent end.

Then, I watched the ripple vibrate over a good friend.

I'm ashamed to say that you slipped my mind,

can't believe 15 years just passed.

15 years since you prepared for a Good Friday.

That turned into your last.

And yes, we've lost too many over the years,

rest Powerfully to my only big bro.

Seems as if since that day we've been falling,

your death the first domino.

I pray your soul is at peace.

I pray you forgave those who caused your tears.

I pray you forgive me for not thinking of you for a few years.

So, the least I can do, is write your name,

as for the world never to forget.

A boy with such a light, he was blinded.

Before he could cross, he got hit.

Before he probably had his first kiss.

Remember all the girls used to diss.

Him because even he had less than me, and sometimes, I didn't have shit.

But I remember that you loved to read!

Ironic how I grew up to write books.

And then, your pain was written and published.

And sometimes, I never took a look.

The universe works in mysterious ways.

I believe that our souls are connected.

Because I feel you in my heart, and your memory is protected.

I remember your voice, and you talked with a slur.

Amazing how time blurs sights seen.

Yet, with you there's no blur.

I pray, Mrs. H, accepted that it was God, it wasn't on her.

She jumped in to try to save you. But God, did not concur.

We sat on the bus for hours, until we found out where you were.

Pulled up at Vine that night, parents waiting, all heart broken, and stirred.

I've never seen life flash, the image forever framed.

Not a picture but engraved in my brain.

I pray that you remain.

I pray that you gain.

I pray the world never forgets your name,

Christopher Drinkard.

What A Daughter Does

I was that little girl, that was born to a boy.

Who loved me a little, but loved the streets more.

The boy to whom I was born, decided to make a choice.

To live a life that could rob him of his life, freedom, and voice.

A boy he was when I was born, a man he never truly came.

For he was only 20, when the guy blew his brains.

And I do mean that literally, he was executed out in the street.

That little girl he took part in, the woman she became he'll never meet.

The woman that little girl became forgives the boy her father was.

Because regardless he is my father, and that's what a daughter does.

Wishing Well

This letter is to the wishing well.

Tossing in my two cents.

Tossing in my prayers for forgiveness.

To my Lord I repent.

Thank you for picking me up tall,

when I fall short.

And I thank you for protecting me, when I made the wrong choice.

But, wishing well, I wish you will, grant me one wish.

I wish for 60 seconds with the ones, that I terribly miss.

I only need one minute, for one hug and one kiss.

For you to point out the snakes, when I'm deaf to the hiss.

For a minute, I'll give my hands, learn to write with my wrist.

Offer my tongue on a platter, learn to speak with a lisp.

Wishing well, I wish you will.

Abort my mistakes from last night, no pill.

Because last night,

with my might,

I had a sight to kill.

Murder, pre-meditated.

POW! POW! No hesitation.

Then I'd be another statistic,

another child that didn't make it.

Another life, gone and wasted.

For being vulnerable, emotions naked.

If the well can't grant me peace, my peace, I'll go take it.

And toss it in the wishing well, with my two cents.

For I know if I keep it, revenge is the risk.

Worst Enemy

I wouldn't wish this on my worst enemy.
The pain nor the tears.

I wouldn't wish the void in their hearts.
That fills mine through the years.

I am blessed for the memories,
I sometimes to pray to forget.

Losing my brother caused a catastrophic event.
My butterfly effect.

Dominos falling.
Left, right, up, and down.

Going crazy like The Joker.
Ironic because even my frown is hidden by my planted smile.

No dark knights,
through my dark nights.

No superhero with a cape.

Been in pain for so long,
I'm beginning to wonder if it was innate.

A blessing or a curse?
I often ask myself.
Screaming to the skies,
begging the Lord for help.

To heal my,
broken heart, broken soul.
Lost dreams, lost goals.
Lasting tears, lasting pain.

To stop me from going out of my mind,
and in-sane.

Don't get me wrong there has been good in my life.
My son being the reason I survive and can see.

Yet, I wouldn't wish my pain on my worst enemy.
Yet, my worst enemy can be me.

Your Honor

There's no honor among the wicked.

Cop pull us over, death before a ticket.

Death before the honor.

Court's Hell, hotter than a sauna.

The Judge, judges me before the judgement,

judges me just for being born.

Feminist tendencies, he's acting like a woman that's been scorned.

He want to burn my clothes, burn my skin, burn my heritage line.

So, he handed me a life sentence, and said, "Your life is mine."

And before I go, I say,

"You're a lie. You can't touch my soul, even if you try. I am proud of my Black skin, and never will I apologize.

But I accept your apology, for all the blood you made bleed. For all the times you uprooted us, trying to kill our seeds. For the Black bodies you made suspend, for hanging my Black kin. Native land was protected, Europeans brought the sin. Soon then, you bought us in. We made the paper, you made the pen. The pen is truly greater than the sword, for the pen we're still locked in.

Locked in cages, entrapped for ages, literally every generation. It's not all your fault, for we have the power, but we're still waiting.

Our freedom is in our hands, not in the white man's. You say I can't be free, I say I can. You say I'm not royalty, I say I am. You say pay Uncle Sam, I'm calling Aunt Pam. My Aunt Pam don't play, for hers, she'll slay. Aunt Pam be the auntie that put more upon your plate. Aunt Pam be the fam, that make sure you say ma'am. If I call Aunt Pam, she'll be the one that brings the Ham.

It's Hammer time. Locked and loaded. If we have to go to war, I'm toting. I see that smirk smile on your face, and does it look like I'm joking?

I know you hoping. That more of us will keep our eyes closed, not open. For if we see the truth, recognize the proof, when we reach our mind, and secure the loot. You know for sure you'll lose. So, you do what you must do. To make sure we stay blind. 400 years behind.

Do you see my signature?

I signed this letter, to you, your honor.

Sealed by the blood of, your founding fathers.

Delivered to those who must be delivered, don't bother.

To try intercept the message, truth no longer neglected.

If one soul must be sacrificed to shed the light, I'll protect it.

And that's

death before dishonor.

Your honor."

Your Melody

I'm old enough to know better, yet too young to know it all.

Many times, I pick up my phone, with nobody to call.

My past made me who I am. Yet, it doesn't dictate who I shall be.

I see where I want to go, yet the path isn't easily seen.

Like I always wanted to be a mom, but I believed my womb could bear no fruit.

But God knew when to implant my seed. SHE knew I would need his lovely roots.

Sometimes it pains me to say, that he's the reason I'm sane.

Yet, happy to declare that because of him, I'll never be the same.

I'll never lay or never stray.

I'll never sleep on my son until our Lord take me away.

Franklin, I promise, mommy will stand tall, until I fall on that day.

And even then, remember that you're my son(sun), with all the brightness and rays.

Never be blinded and always sing to your own tune.

And as your melody will beat through your heart,

Remember that my heartbeat is

YOU!

WORDS OF REFLECTION

More Books By Chanekka Pullens

-The Book About M.E.: Mind Elevation

-The Poetry Book About M.E.: Melanin Experience

Princess Lu Children's Book Series

-Nice To Meet You, Princess Lu!

-Celebrate Black History Month With Princess Lu!

-Princess Lu Teaches Juan His ABC's

Connect With Me

Facebook.com/mindelevationforallfan

Instagram: @elevationforall

Twitter: @elevationforall

About the author

Chanekka Pullens is the proud mother of Juan, 2. She graduated from Middle Tennessee State University in 2015. She received her bachelor's degree in Political Science with a double minor in History and International Relations. She published her first book, "The Book About M.E.: Mind Elevation" in 2014. Her first poetry book, "The Poetry Book About M.E.: Melanin Experience" was published in 2017. Read more about Chanekka, her books, and her Princess Lu Children's Book Series at: www.mindelevationforall.org.

www.ingramcontent.com/pod-product-compliance
Lightning Source LLC
Chambersburg PA
CBHW071232090426
42736CB00014B/3059